Richard Scarry's
First Little Learners

From
1 to 10

Can you help
Miss Honey
count to ten?

Of course,
you can!

One

MARCHING BAGPIPER

TWO

FRIENDLY POLICEMEN

Three
BUSY ARTISTS

Four
SPEEDY MOTORBOATS

Five
FUNNY SAILORS

6

Six
COLORFUL KITES

13

Seven

FIRE ENGINES

Eight

LITTLE AIRPLANES

9

Nine

HAPPY MAIL CARRIERS

Ten

GREAT BIG GRUMPY GUARDS!